Hello!

By Janine Amos

Illustrated by Annabel Spenceley

CHERRYTREE BOOKS

A Cherrytree Book

Designed and produced
by A S Publishing

First published in 1998
by Cherrytree Books
a division of the Evans Publishing Group
2A Portman Mansions
Chiltern St
London W1U 6NR

Reprinted 2002 (twice), 2004

British Library Cataloguing in Publication Data

Amos, Janine
  Hello!. – (Good manners)
  1.Interpersonal relations – Juvenile literature
  I.Title II.Spenceley, Annabel
  395.1'22

ISBN 1 84234 121 9

Printed in Malaysia

David's kite

David is going to the park with Dad.

They meet a neighbour.

Dad stops to say Hello.

David is thinking of the park.
He does not answer.

How does Mr Hill feel?

9

David thinks about it.

On the way back, David remembers.

How does **Mr Hill** feel now?

Emma and Sita

Emma is hanging up her coat.

Sita dashes in. She wants to get started.

Emma is pleased to see Sita.

Sita forgets to say Hello.

How does Emma feel?

Sita remembers. She turns round.

How does Emma feel now?

Jon joins in

Jamie is playing with the others.

Jon comes along.

Jon watches the game.
He wants to join in.

Jamie sees Jon watching.

Jamie calls to Jon.

How does Jon feel?

Jon joins in the game.

31

"People like to be greeted. When you meet someone you know, make them feel welcome. Greet them with a smile and say Hello. If a friend says Hello to you, remember to greet them in return."